DIESELS IN THE HIGHLANDS

Andrew Vines

Ian Allan
PUBLISHING

First published 2006

ISBN (10) 0 7110 3118 5
ISBN (13) 978 0 7110 3118 0

© Andrew Vines 2006

Published by Ian Allan Publishing

an imprint of Ian Allan Publishing Ltd, Hersham, Surrey KT12 4RG
Printed in England by Ian Allan Printing Ltd, Hersham, Surrey KT12 4RG

Code: 0608/B1

Visit the Ian Allan Publishing website at www.ianallanpublishing.com

Front cover: Against a background of Beinn Odhar, Class 37/4 No 37425
Sir Robert McAlpine / Concrete Bob heads downhill towards Bridge of
Orchy with the late-running 16.50 Glasgow–Fort William on 18 June 1987.
Andrew Vines

Back cover: Class 47/4 No 47462 accelerates away from Pitlochry with the
14.30 Inverness–Edinburgh on 26 September 1987. *Andrew Vines*

Introduction

Threading their way across wild and remote landscapes, from Craigendoran in the south to Caithness in the far north, the spectacular railways of the Scottish Highlands, possess their own distinct identity. This book covers the four main rail routes in the area. Firstly, the West Highland: famous almost from the day it opened in 1894, it is *the* quintessential rail route through the region. There is something of an epic quality in its passage of the glens and lochs, the crossing of Rannoch Moor and the descent to Lochaber, before the extension onward to the coast at Mallaig. Secondly, the Highland line from Perth to Inverness: this is the only true main line in the Highlands, encompassing a remarkable variety of scenery and including the highest point on the national rail network. Beyond Inverness, the route to the far north at first runs through the farmlands of Easter Ross, but when it turns inland towards Lairg and again through the Strath of Kildonan it takes on a bleak and lonely trek through desolate country, although it never quite seems to reach the scenic high-points of the other routes. Lastly the Kyle line, which, after striking west from Dingwall across the bleak interior, descends to the beautiful shoreline of Loch Carron to provide some of the finest combinations of mountains and seascape to be seen by rail, and a fitting finale to this journey. This scenic background provides the theme of this book. It is the outstanding quality of the landscape which gives the railways of the Highlands their own individual appeal, and the pictures chosen here unashamedly reflect this. Those seeking close-up shots of locomotive detail will have to look elsewhere.

Diesels arrived early in British Railways' Modernisation Programme, and by the end of 1962 the takeover from steam was all but complete. A variety of Type 2s predominated, but for many years operating practices changed little, and the diesels simply worked in a steam-age environment. Miraculously the basic network survived the Beeching era, with the exception of the Callander and Oban route east of Crianlarich, which to some extent duplicated the southern end of the West Highland line. However, it was not until the early 1970s, when the fight to save the Kyle line was won, that the threat of rail closures in the Highlands was finally lifted. An increase in traffic to Inverness and beyond, which resulted from exploration for North Sea oil, seemed to underline the change in fortunes.

From then on the railways looked forward to a more assured future, and the latter part of the decade saw an increasing use of larger motive power in the form of Classes 37 and 47, replacing the Type 2s which had dominated for so long. Nevertheless, real change began only in the 1980s, when the Highland lines found themselves at the forefront of innovation through the introduction of radio signalling, which replaced traditional semaphores and signalboxes, initially on the Kyle line and then on the Far North and West Highland routes. At the same time an outward-looking and enterprising Scottish Region management led by Chris Green began to win increased local backing and investment for their railways. 'ScotRail' was launched as a brand name, stations were refurbished and others reopened, whilst the whole railway environment took on a more optimistic air. The limit of Central Government commitment to the Highlands' railways was, however, demonstrated in the failed saga to add a rail crossing to the new Dornoch road bridge, which would have enabled trains to the far north to compete on better terms with the road.

An experimental devolved management structure based on local decision-making was the cue for a plethora of enterprising initiatives. The revival of summer steam to Mallaig was the most high-profile, but there were many others. Observation cars were reintroduced to Kyle and Mallaig, along with more unusual ventures such as 'ETHELs' (Electric Train Heat Ex-Locomotives) converted from Class 25s to heat

Previous page: Class 47/4 No 47517 *Andrew Carnegie* wheels the southbound 'Clansman' (10.30 Inverness–Euston) past Glentruim, near Newtonmore, amid the autumn tints on 23 October 1987. *Andrew Vines*

Right: High above Loch Carron, on the Kyle line, the peace of a fine summer's evening is intermittently disturbed by the sound of a train making its way down the shoreline around the succession of bays and inlets. Briefly it emerges from behind a rock face and calls at Duncraig Halt, below its attendant castle, before moving on down the lochside towards Kyle. Class 37/4 No 37417 *Highland Region* heads the 17.55 from Inverness on 16 June 1987. *Andrew Vines*

the Fort William sleeper during the changeover period from steam to electric heating. Freight flourished under the Speedlink revival, with colourful wagons making up numerous 'Enterprise' and trip workings of timber and other products. Tourist trips suddenly found a new market in 1985 with the arrival of the luxury 'Royal Scotsman' cruising train, quickly followed by several imitators. Colourful and eye-catching locomotive liveries multiplied with the abandonment of corporate blue, all enhanced by evocative Scottish names and personalised depot motifs applied at Eastfield and Inverness. It all made for a colourful and interesting period for the enthusiast, the like of which had not been seen for decades, and the pictures in this book centre on this relatively brief period.

It couldn't last, of course. Firstly, in an effort to cut costs, management was re-centralised. Then came the necessary economy of 'Sprinter' operation, which in 1989 largely replaced locomotive haulage on the West Highland and Far North lines, the Kyle line and the Highland main line following a few years later. The abandonment in 1991 of the Speedlink network initially saw a drastic reduction in freight in the Highlands, only Fort William's staple traffic in paper and aluminium surviving the cull. One by one the luxury trains disappeared, leaving only the most enduring, the 'Royal Scotsman', whilst locomotive-hauled passenger trains were finally removed from the summer timetables in the countdown to full privatisation.

Since then the picture has been mixed. Devolution has seen the Scottish Executive exhibit a refreshing commitment to its railways, in contrast to the traditional political indifference further south. Sterling efforts have been made at the local level, mainly through the setting-up of the Highland Rail Partnership, and some success has been achieved, particularly on the freight side. However, the almost continual process of losses and gains in commodities serves to demonstrate the constant effort required to compete with road haulage. The privatised passenger services have been run with economy, and have seen limited expansion, but seemingly with no desire to find an imaginative way of exploiting the lines' tourist potential in summer, beyond the well-established steam operation to Mallaig. Surely something more inspiring than 'Sprinters' could be found to draw the summer crowds and lift the whole tourist experience on the West Highland and Kyle lines? These are our most outstanding scenic railways by far; a journey on the West Highland or the Kyle line ranks with any in the world, and it must be hoped that, with enterprise and commitment, they will continue to operate successfully for many decades to come.

Acknowledgements
The Highlands is the most rewarding area for scenic railway photography, despite the vagaries of the weather and the paucity of trains. My thanks to Antony, Hugh, John and Les, who have willingly contributed pictures where time, rain, midges and my own inabilities have left gaps in my collection.

Andrew Vines
January 2006

Right: With frozen points all over the network and the timetable in tatters the morning after Boxing Day, a very late-running 'Sprinter' forming the 08.12 Glasgow–Mallaig crosses the County March summit north of Tyndrum in a swirl of snow during the big freeze of 1995. It was so cold that day that at Bridge of Orchy temperatures reached a *maximum* of –10°C! *Andrew Vines*

Below: Christmas on the West Highland: Ardlui, 1995. *Andrew Vines*

On a warm summer afternoon Class 37/4 No 37412 *Loch Lomond* runs into Ardlui, at the foot of Glen Falloch, with the 12.56 Fort William–Mossend freight, mostly comprising VDA vans in red and grey Speedlink livery, in June 1987. Class 37s were first tried on the West Highland for a few weeks in the spring of 1968, but the perennial problem of tyre wear on the sharp curves put paid to the experiment. It was to be another decade before they appeared again, and this time they were here to stay. *Andrew Vines*

Class 37/4 No 37402 *Oor Wullie* leaves Ardlui with a down freight on 18 June 1987. Ben Lomond is the distant peak. On this occasion the train continued only as far as Crianlarich, to be stabled on the spur to the old Crianlarich Lower station for picking-up a day or so later by a locomotive and crew from the opposite end of the line. The stabling of freights at intermediate stations was once a common practice when a corresponding working was unavailable from the opposite direction to permit the swapping of train crews. *Andrew Vines*

Autumn in the Highlands produces a dazzling array of colours far exceeding those generally seen further south. In this scene beside Loch Etive Class 37/4 No 37401 *Mary Queen of Scots*, the first of the class to carry InterCity livery, nears Connel Ferry on 2 November 1988 with the 09.45 Mossend–Oban freight.

The train is made up entirely of oil tankers — one each for the Shell depot at Connel Ferry and the BP depot on the quayside next to Oban station, the remainder destined for the Esso depot on the site once occupied by Oban's locomotive depot. *Andrew Vines*

Class 37/4 No 37406 *The Saltire Society*, heading the 12.50 Oban–Glasgow
Queen Street service, thuds over the girders of the Orchy Viaduct, at the head of
Loch Awe, on the same beautiful afternoon as the picture opposite. *Andrew Vines*

Left: The Oban line is not short on scenic attraction, although it is frequently overlooked in favour of the route to Fort William. Against a background of snow-capped Ben Cruachan Class 37/4 No 37405 *Strathclyde Region* noses around the shoreline of Loch Etive near Achnacloich with the lunchtime Oban–Glasgow service on 20 February 1987. *Andrew Vines*

Right: Perhaps the most famous section of the West Highland line is the 'horseshoe' curve, north of Tyndrum, where the railway takes a dramatic 'U'-shaped course around Auch Glen, skirting the base of three mountains in turn and crossing the intervening valleys on viaducts. The mountains are suddenly at close quarters, towering above the train, in contrast to much of the journey to Fort William where the hills are seen at a distance across the glens and lochs. Here Class 37/4 No 37403 *Isle of Mull* exits the north side of the curve with the 09.50 Glasgow–Fort William on 31 January 1987. The train is rounding the base of Beinn Dorain and is backed by the looming bulk of Beinn a'Chaisteil, the lower slopes of which it has just traversed. *Andrew Vines*

Highest, wildest and most remote of all the West Highland stations is Corrour, on the northern edge of Rannoch Moor. Surrounded by the mountain ranges of west central Scotland, it is surely one of the least accessible stations in Britain, being more than seven miles from the nearest public road. In this view, recorded on

25 April 1981, Class 27/1 No 27106 approaches with the morning Mallaig–Glasgow service as a special from Glasgow to Glenfinnan, organised by the photographer and headed by Class 27/0 No 27 034, waits for the road north. *John Spencer Gilks*

Class 27s had a long association with the West Highland, dominating the motive power for two decades following their first appearances in 1961, save for a period in the late 1960s when Paxman-engined North British Type 2s (Class 29) predominated. Here No 27032 ascends Glen Falloch with the 08.06 Glasgow–Oban on the morning of 11 April 1979. The type's final appearance on the line is believed to have been in July 1987, when, perhaps to commemorate the passing of an era, No 27005 piloted a Class 37 on a train of alumina tanks just before the class became extinct. *Les Nixon*

13

Above: On the fine winter's afternoon of 18 February 1987 Class 37/4 No 37407 *Loch Long* heads away from Crianlarich towards Tyndrum Lower with the 12.20 Glasgow–Oban, with the twin peaks of Ben More (left) and Stob Binnein in the background. *Andrew Vines*

Right: Early on a winter's morning the first rays of weak sunshine illuminate the side of Class 37/4 No 37405 *Strathclyde Region*, seen nearing Bridge of Orchy with the 05.10 Mossend–Fort William freight on 31 January 1987. Following a night of severe cold the frost on the roof of the leading van has been only partially melted by eddying heat from the locomotive's exhaust. *Andrew Vines*

Sheltering under the deep hollow of Coire an Dothaidh, Bridge of Orchy is an 'oasis' among the mountains, comprising nothing more than a station, an hotel and a few houses. It was the existence of the hotel, together with the old military road which crossed the line at this point, that gave the West Highland Railway the thinnest of excuses to build a station. For trains there are sustained climbs both southwards to County March Summit and northwards to Gorton, on Rannoch Moor. In former times railway staff undertook postal duties; now the station has been usefully converted into a bunkhouse for walkers and climbers.

These four pictures show Bridge of Orchy through the seasons: the pale yellows of spring *(left)* give way to the greens of summer *(below)*, followed by the flame red grasses of autumn *(right)* and, finally, the snows of winter *(below right)*. The pictures were taken in May 1994, June 1990, November 1990 and December 1995 respectively. *Andrew Vines*

Seen north of Bridge of Orchy on 30 May 1985, Class 37 No 37263 has 'ETHEL 2' in tow with the morning sleeper to Fort William. The introduction from October 1983 of the three 'ETHEL' electric heating units, converted at Aberdeen Ferryhill depot for this service, was a unique and characterful exercise which seemed to sum up the enterprising spirit evident within ScotRail at the time.

After the West Highland had no further use for them they spent several more years providing heat for steam specials, their appearance often offending the æsthetic sensibilities of steam photographers, before being consigned to the scrapyard in the early 1990s. *Les Nixon*

The 'ETHELs' were only a temporary expedient for the sleeper until the arrival of Class 37/4s, which gradually began to take over West Highland services in the latter half of 1985. Specially converted to provide electric train heating, they allowed ScotRail to dispense with steam heating in the Highlands — and very soon afterwards from the entire system. Here No 37428 *Loch Awe / Loch Long*, in 'Royal Scotsman' livery, heads the sleeper across the Garbh Ghaoir Viaduct, in the midst of Rannoch Moor, as the morning mist rises from the distant hills in July 2003. *Andrew Vines*

19

Above: Nowadays it is difficult to imagine the fuss created when Allan Baker, Depot Engineer at Eastfield, painted a white stripe along the sides of some of his Class 37s (plus a Class 27) in 1983. Senior management frowned on the idea, and they were removed within a few weeks of this picture, such was the continuing grip of the corporate image on BR, even in the early 1980s. An evening crossing at Crianlarich on 14 May 1984 sees No 37081 *Loch Long* waiting with the southbound bauxite empties from Fort William to North Blyth whilst No 37037 enters the station with the 13.30 Mossend–Oban oil tanks, both locomotives exhibiting the stripe as well as the small version of the West Highland terrier motif. It was the intention at one time to name No 37037 *'Loch Treig'*, but in 1986 the locomotive was transferred from Eastfield to Motherwell for steel duties, becoming 37321 *Gartcosh*. Following numerous further changes and eventual withdrawal No 37037 would be preserved on the South Devon Railway, where it would not only regained its white stripe but also be given its rightful name, *Loch Treig*. *Hugh Dady*

Right: Twilight of the Fort William sleeper? Cotton grass bobs in the late-evening breeze at Corrour as Class 37/4 No 37428 *Loch Awe / Loch Long* passes the battered remains of the summit boards with the up service to Euston on 4 July 2003. The West Highland sleeper service has been under threat of withdrawal several times in recent years and by the dawn of the new millennium appeared something of an anachronism on a railway dominated by multiple-units and General Motors power. However, the survival of all the Scottish sleepers has become something of a political issue in recent years, and, with the more favourable attitude adopted by the Scottish Executive towards railways in general, the West Highland sleeper may yet have a long-term future. *Andrew Vines*

Right: The old North British lattice-post signals which once graced the West Highland's stations were largely swept away early in 1986, when locomotive-operated points were installed prior to the introduction of radio signalling. Fortunately Mallaig Junction, just outside Fort William, retained its steam-age infrastructure, including the semaphore signals and 'box, which still survive at the time of writing. Here Class 37/4 No 37405 *Strathclyde Region* has been checked on the approach to the junction before accelerating over the pointwork on the last lap into the station with the 16.34 from Glasgow Queen Street on 8 June 1988. Mallaig Junction had just been renamed 'Fort William Junction' to avoid confusion when giving messages via the radio signalling equipment. *Andrew Vines*

Below: A Class 08 shunter had been stationed at Fort William since the early 1960s, but in the 1980s it was replaced by a Class 20, the increased power being useful for local trip workings. At Mallaig Junction yard on 13 May 1988 No 20138 shunts a single oil tank, retrieved from the station after arriving empty from Mallaig the day before. This was one of only three Class 20s fitted with the radio equipment necessary for working on the West Highland. At the end of the decade the '20' was again replaced by an '08', before the area lost its shunter altogether. *Andrew Vines*

Right: Mallaig in April 1989 graphically illustrates the vast improvement in road communications at the expense of rail. The station and approach tracks once occupied prime position next to the foreshore, a position now taken up by the reconstructed A830 road; the much-reduced station is sandwiched between the road and the town. Class 37/4 No 37409 *Loch Awe* runs around the stock of an InterCity charter as snow showers gather over the wild country to the north. The shortened station loop complicates shunting manœuvres, the nine-coach train being split into two; one part is in the siding adjacent to the station, the other on the 'main' line behind the photographer. *Andrew Vines*

Below: Dramatic lighting conditions at Loch Eil Outward Bound on the evening of 22 April 1989. The 18.15 Mallaig–Glasgow Class 156 unit departs against a backdrop of snow-clad Ben Nevis, three months after 'Sprinters' took over most West Highland passenger services from the Class 37s. The halt was opened in April 1985 to serve the adjacent outdoor centre. *Andrew Vines*

Right: In early summer photography in the Highlands is possible late into the evening. On 17 June 1987 Class 37/4 No 37425 *Sir Robert McAlpine / Concrete Bob* catches the last rays of evening sun on the Lochy Viaduct outside Fort William, prior to a twilight trip through the glens with the 21.05 to Mallaig. Unusually the train includes the fuel-oil tankers (for Mallaig's fishing fleet) normally attached to the teatime service. *Andrew Vines*

Class 37/4 No 37422 climbs slowly beside the narrows of Loch Eilt with the 18.45 Mallaig–Fort William 'mixed' service on 8 June 1988. With many of the best viewpoints at some distance from the road and with long gaps between trains, photography on the Mallaig line could be a leisurely business, allowing time to take in the scenery and enjoy such delights as fresh salmon from the nearby Lochailort Inn. However, all that changed in the evening, when the sun moved around, opening up a series of roadside views which meant that this, the last train of the day from Mallaig, could be chased between locations, often involving some hair-raising driving manœuvres to boot! *Andrew Vines*

Rain and steam at Glenfinnan: Class 37/0 No 37191 *International Youth Year 1985* arrives during an evening downpour on 25 May 1985 with the 18.50 Mallaig–Fort William 'mixed' service, in weather far more typical of the Western Highlands than most of the other pictures in this book! Mixed trains operated in various parts of the Highlands in the diesel era, but the regular use of passenger trains to convey fuel tanks was unique to the Mallaig line. No doubt today's safety-conscious authorities would be horrified at the prospect of marshalling loaded oil tanks next to a passenger-carrying vehicle. *Andrew Vines*

Left: Locomotive-hauled passenger trains made a temporary return to the Mallaig extension in 1992, when 'Sprinter' units were reallocated elsewhere for the duration of the summer. Class 37/4 No 37406 *The Saltire Society* heads the 16.05 Fort William–Mallaig alongside the inaccessible southern shore of Loch Eilt near the abandoned cottage at Essan on the afternoon of 4 July. *Andrew Vines*

Right: The Mallaig train winds its way around the rock faces west of Lochailort. Here Class 37/4 No 37425 *Sir Robert McAlpine / Concrete Bob* heads the 16.10 from Fort William on 17 June 1987. Just yards from this location the new Mallaig road has been blasted through the landscape at great public expense, in the process destroying the once tranquil scene at the head of Loch Ailort. Like many other members of the class this locomotive ranged far and wide after leaving Scotland in 1989 and exhibited a variety of colour schemes, but in 2005 it was returned to 'large logo' livery to mark the end of locomotive-hauled services on the Rhymney branch in South Wales. *Andrew Vines*

Left: In the 1980s Fort William's resident Class 20 occasionally strayed from the shunting environs of Lochaber to substitute for a Class 37, usually on the teatime 'school' service to Mallaig. On one such occasion, 8 July 1987, No 20208 heads upgrade from Keppoch Moss towards Arisaig near Kinloid, with the return 18.50 Mallaig–Fort William. *Antony Guppy*

Right: The appearance in 1989 of the Chipman and Schering weed-control trains, powered by privately owned Hunslet-Barclay Class 20/9s, provided a touch of variety on the railways in a year of increasing standardisation. On 19 July the Chipman train visited the Oban line and is seen approaching Connel Ferry with No 20901 leading and No 20904 bringing up the rear. The train returned to Crianlarich in the afternoon before continuing to Fort William; the following morning it visited Mallaig. *Andrew Vines*

Left: The viaducts of the Mallaig line are well known for their early use of mass concrete. Early on 20 May 1985 Class 37/0 No 37011 slips across the head of Loch nan Uamh ('the Loch of the Caves') with the 06.50 Mallaig–Fort William. The area is rich in the history of Bonnie Prince Charlie, who, after hiding from the English following the defeat of the Jacobite uprising at Culloden, fled Scotland forever from the shores of Loch nan Uamh in September 1745. A present-day roadside cairn marks the spot. Rather more prosaically, No 37011 would come to a premature end following a collision with an electric unit at Singer in January 1987, becoming only the second of the class to be withdrawn. *Andrew Vines*

Above: Class 37/0 No 37033 leaves Morar on the 06.50 Mallaig–Fort William service on 22 May 1985. Like the LNER 'K2s' before them, several Class 37s were plucked from an anonymous life in East Anglia, given various Eastfield embellishments (including names for some) and put to work on the West Highland. No 37033 had a typically varied life: having moved from March to Eastfield in 1981, it would become the last of the 1980s programme of heavy general overhauls at Crewe works, emerging in 1989 as '37/7' No 37719, allocated to a South Wales Metals pool. It would be placed in store in 1999, albeit ostensibly remaining available for contract hire in France some seven years later. *Andrew Vines*

Left: No 37425 again, this time drifting down the glen of the Abhainn Shlatach towards Glenfinnan with the 18.50 Mallaig–Fort William in June 1987. *Andrew Vines*

Below: Late on the evening of 5 June 1991 No 37428 *David Lloyd George*, in Petroleum Sub-sector livery, heads the 16.38 Corpach–Mossend freight southwards from Crianlarich towards the head of Glen Falloch. The attraction of the scene in print is tempered by the memory of being plagued at the time by that curse of Highland summers, the Scottish midge. The sight of a hapless victim out in the open, trying to ward off the 'wee beasties' with characteristically wild and involuntary thrashing movements, is a sight immediately recognisable to anyone who has been similarly afflicted! *Andrew Vines*

Left: On a day of dazzling sunshine interspersed with sudden snow showers an equally bright Class 37/4 No 37409 *Loch Awe*, on its first outing after repaint in InterCity livery, climbs from Keppoch Moss to Arisaig with a 'West Highlander' InterCity charter returning southwards on 23 April 1989. *Andrew Vines*

Below: It has become something of a tradition in recent years for the Scottish Railway Preservation Society to run an excursion to Mallaig in early May, and more often than not the weather is favourable. Saturday 4 May 2002 was no exception as Class 37/4s Nos 37415 and 37405 climbed away from Achallader with a day trip to Mallaig which had begun at Dunbar at 05.30. In many ways this scene sums up the West Highland, with the train on a hillside climbing north towards the Moor of Rannoch, set against a beautiful landscape of mountains, moor and loch. *Andrew Vines*

Left: On the Highland main line north of Dunkeld, No 47563 *Woman's Guild* hauls a rake of alternate coach liveries forming the northbound 'Clansman' (08.55 Euston–Inverness) near Dalguise in June 1987. The 'Clansman' was introduced in 1974 as the first regular daytime service between Inverness and London and was made possible by the speeding-up of services following electrification of the West Coast main line. It also brought the first, temporary allocation of a Class 47 to Inverness, presaging the eventual demise of Type 2s on the Highland

main line. The train itself would eventually be withdrawn following the widespread introduction of 'Sprinters' on the route. *Andrew Vines*

Above: The old order on the Highland main line: Class 26/1 No 26026 (in Railfreight grey livery) and Class 20 No 20114 double-head the 18.20 Inverness–Mossend freight through Strath Tay, near Guay, on 1 June 1987. *Andrew Vines*

Left: The general abandonment of push-pull working on Glasgow, Edinburgh and Aberdeen services in May 1990 resulted in the widespread use of Class 47/7s on Inverness services for a time. Deep in the Pass of Killiecrankie, No 47710 *Sir Walter Scott* crosses Killiecrankie Viaduct, close to the 'Soldier's Leap' over the River Garry, with the 12.10 Edinburgh–Inverness on 24 May 1990. The first coach is a stray from Network SouthEast, sent north after the disbanding of several locomotive-hauled rakes. *Andrew Vines*

Right: By the date of this picture, 2 June 1987, the Class 26s had been relegated to a secondary role on the Highland main line. No 26036 drifts down from Druimuachdar to Dalwhinnie with the early-morning Millerhill–Inverness Speedlink freight service, past a photographic viewpoint since spoiled by a line of wires erected between the river and the railway. *Andrew Vines*

Left: Druimuachdar Pass in summer: Class 37/0 No 37068 *Grainflow* is on the last mile to the summit with the 03.45 Millerhill–Inverness Speedlink freight, which appropriately includes 'Grainflow' wagons travelling from East Anglia to the Burghead branch, on 14 June 1988. Other traffic consists of cement from Oxwellmains and LPG tanks from Grangemouth to Inverness. All would subsequently be lost to the railway with the demise of Speedlink in 1991, but cement traffic to Inverness has since returned as part of the freight revival on the privatised railway.
Andrew Vines

Right: A few minutes after the previous photograph the southbound 'Highland Chieftain' HST sweeps over the summit with power car No 43194 leading. Introduced in May 1984 and originally envisaged as a summer-only supplement to the West Coast 'Clansman', the train has become a permanent fixture in the timetable and provides a relatively fast early-morning service to the Scottish and English capitals, as well as an afternoon return.
Andrew Vines

Druimuachdar in winter: having just passed the summit — at 1,484ft the highest point on the national rail network — Class 47/4 No 47461 *Charles Rennie Mackintosh* begins the descent towards Dalwhinnie with the 12.33 Glasgow–Inverness in February 1987. The improved A9 road and the presence of the electricity pylons have reduced the feeling of remoteness which must have existed in 1863, when the Inverness & Perth Junction Railway first pushed its route through this, the most obvious pass through the central Grampians. *Andrew Vines*

Against a backdrop of the snow-mantled Grampians Class 47/4 No 47578 *The Royal Society of Edinburgh* gathers speed on the descent of upper Glen Garry with the 12.30 Inverness–Edinburgh on 17 February 1987. This section of line between Blair Atholl and Dalwhinnie was singled in July 1966 as part of an economy drive, only to be doubled again in April 1978 to accommodate the growth in traffic resulting from North Sea oil. *Andrew Vines*

The skirl o' the pipes in Glen Garry! Class 37/4 No 37401 *Mary Queen of Scots* and '37/5' No 37682 *Hartlepool Pipe Mill* crawl up the long grade from Blair Atholl with a trainload of pipes from Hartlepool to Georgemas Junction on the morning of 29 August 1996. This exceptionally heavy train, loaded to some 1,000 tons, is down to no more than 20mph crossing the bridge over the River Garry, the thin haze of exhaust giving a clue to the noise and effort involved.

This was only the second occasion on which this particular train had run; on the first a single Class 37 had predictably come to grief on the gradients of the Highland main line, but this time sanity prevailed, and No 37401 was added at Millerhill. Pipe traffic for use in the North Sea oil and gas industries has been conveyed intermittently by the railway to and from various railheads in the north of Scotland since the 1970s. *Hugh Dady*

Class 37/4 No 37405 *Strathclyde Region* on the long curve south of Dalwhinnie with the northbound 'Royal Scotsman' heading for Boat of Garten, just after 8pm on 24 May 1990. The beautiful evening light and spotless condition of the train are unfortunately not matched by the state of the locomotive, which is adorned with a veneer of brown brake dust, a symptom of Eastfield depot's lack of proper washing facilities. The stock is the later 'Royal Scotsman' rake, made up largely of Metro-Cammell former Pullman cars and introduced that year. Regrettably the nice former Great Northern teak coach, second from front, is no longer in use.
Andrew Vines

The ubiquitous General Motors Class 66 has now invaded the Highlands, just as it has every other part of the rail network. EWS No 66102 heads southwards near Crubenmore, between Newtonmore and Dalwhinnie with a permanent-way train returning from Inverness to Millerhill yard on 7 May 2002. *Andrew Vines*

A high-profile example of the partial revival of freight traffic in the Highlands following privatisation was the conveyance by EWS of intermodal containers for the Safeway supermarket chain from Glasgow to Inverness, commencing in 1999 and later extended to the far north. The empty southbound containers are seen here forming part of the 15.12 Inverness–Mossend freight descending Glen Garry near

Dalnaspidal on 4 July 2003. The train was unusually diagrammed for a Class 67 (in this case No 67012) — a type seeking gainful employment following the loss of the Royal Mail contract. Unfortunately subsequent supermarket takeovers would bring a swift end to the Safeway traffic, some five years after its introduction. *Andrew Vines*

The climb from Inverness to the summit at Slochd Mor (1,315ft) — some 20 miles at gradients mostly between 1 in 60 and 1 in 70 — is a daunting prospect for southbound trains. The heavy overnight sleepers must have been some of the toughest duties for the Class 47s, loading up to 15 vehicles (or more) out of Inverness.

In the days when the Highland capital still had two overnight services to London a somewhat lighter load forming the 19.05 (Saturdays) Inverness–Euston, hauled by '47/4' No 47460, completes the climb beside a deserted A9 on 2 June 1990. *Andrew Vines*

The Class 37s went out in style on the Highland main line in the early 1990s by double-heading the Inverness sleeper for a couple of years or so, before their use on regular passenger trains all but finished. Class 37/0 No 37255 and '37/5'

No 37683 lead the 'Royal Highlander' (21.05 ex Euston) around the curves at Balsporran Cottages, north of Druimuachdar, just after 7am on 20 May 1994. *Andrew Vines*

Below: Class 47/4 No 47617 *University of Stirling*, heading the 09.33 Glasgow–Inverness, passes a blaze of lineside colour on the climb from Carrbridge to Slochd on 23 October 1987. *Andrew Vines*

Right: The Highland Railway's new, shorter line from Aviemore to Inverness opened in 1898 and effectively demoted the original route via Forres to a secondary role. The new line was notable for the construction of two enormous viaducts, at Culloden, and across the valley of the Findhorn at Tomatin. The latter is seen here on the afternoon of 23 October 1987 being crossed by Class 47/4 No 47631 on an Inverness–Millerhill Speedlink freight. *Andrew Vines*

Left: Inverness is not only the 'capital' of the Highlands but also the centre for the region's rail operations. Prior to the resignalling scheme of 1986/7 it was probably best known for its fine collection of semaphore signals and gantries, seen in this view of Class 08 No 08717 shunting coaching stock at Welsh's Bridge on 17 April 1986. The new signalling centre, controlling both radio and conventional signalling in the area, would be formally opened on 3 June 1987. The semaphore signals have long gone, but the station retains its unusual triangular layout with platforms on two sides and an avoiding line — the Rose Street curve — on the third. *Les Nixon*

Right: Representatives of the two classes which dominated locomotive haulage in the Highlands throughout the 1980s and '90s — Nos 37424 *Isle of Mull* and 47460 — stand by the fuelling-point at Inverness on 8 September 1990. *Andrew Vines*

Far right: Class 37/0 No 37114 *Dunrobin Castle* climbs up from Invershin towards Lairg on the morning of 16 June 1987 with the 07.18 (Tuesdays and Fridays only) Inverness–Lairg oil tanks. In the background stands Carbisdale Castle above the Kyle of Sutherland. Built in the early 20th century for the Dowager Duchess of Sutherland, it is now a very grand youth hostel, complete with a collection of marble statues and obligatory ghost. *Andrew Vines*

The long-disused station at The Mound closed in 1960 along with several others on the Far North line. It was once the junction for Dornoch, to which Highland Railway 0-4-4 tanks shuffled off twice a day on a very lean service, whilst on the 'main' line restaurant cars lay over here between north- and southbound services. The course of the old branch can be seen curving off to the right in this view recorded on 24 April 1982. Class 26/1 No 26041, heading a special returning from Wick to Inverness, makes an unplanned call, the photographer (who had organised the train) having been assured by railway staff that the inhabitants of the converted station would be out for the afternoon! *John Spencer Gilks*

No 37114 runs round the Lairg tanks on arrival at its destination. The oil depot here serves far-flung areas of the remote North West by onward road distribution, and happily, following a long period of disuse after the collapse of the Ness Viaduct at Inverness in February 1989, the sidings now receive regular rail deliveries again.

Variations in station architecture on the Far North line largely reflect the different phases of the line's construction. Lairg, like the buildings at Invershin and Rogart on the section opened in 1868, appears to have more in common with a crofter's cottage than a railway station. *Andrew Vines*

Left: A bird's-eye view of Class 26/1 No 26033 climbing through Strath Fleet west of Rogart (visible in the distance) with the 11.45 Wick/Thurso–Inverness on 1 June 1981. The '26s' enjoyed a long association with the Far North and Kyle lines, from 1961 to 1984, before the introduction of RETB saw their replacement by Class 37/0s. *Les Nixon*

Below: It is a curiosity of the Far North line that it takes an improbably circuitous route. As well as circumnavigating several estuaries, it twice heads inland for substantial sections of the journey before turning back towards the coast. The idea at the time of building was to help open up the interior, but it has left a legacy of train services which cannot compete on equal terms with the end-to-end timings of buses. On one of the inland sections south of Lairg Class 37/4 No 37417 *Highland Region* heads northwards with the 06.35 Inverness–Wick/Thurso in June 1987. *Andrew Vines*

Below: In contrast with the situation on other Highland lines, on which locomotive-hauled passenger trains continued to make intermittent appearances for several years, the introduction in 1989 of 'Sprinters' on the Far North line saw locomotives permanently banished from the passenger timetable. On an otherwise overcast 27 June 1997 a pair of Class 156 units forming the 17.15 Inverness–Wick service find a patch of sun beside the North Sea between Brora and Helmsdale. The Metro-Cammell Class 156s were perhaps the most successful of BR's 'Sprinter' generation of multiple-units and were much more popular at Inverness than the Class 158s which later replaced them. *Hugh Dady*

Right: Passengers take a last look at the North Sea as Class 37/4 No 37419 approaches the small fishing port of Helmsdale with the 06.35 Inverness–Wick/Thurso on the autumnal morning of 24 October 1987. '37/4s' had begun to replace '37/0s' on Kyle and Far North passenger services from the start of 1986. *Andrew Vines*

Above: Out of the landscape across the sweeping plains of Caithness comes the impressive sight of Class 37/0s Nos 37170 and 37152 heading towards Georgemas Junction with the empty stock of a 'Cock o' the North' InterCity land-cruise train on the evening of 2 May 1993. It later departed southwards for Tain, where the passengers would spend the night on the train before returning to England the following day. *Andrew Vines*

Right: The same train as seen on page 61 leaves Forsinard and sets out on a lone trek across the Flow Country, a vast expanse of featureless peat bog on the borders of Sutherland and Caithness. Forsinard stands near the headwaters of Strath Halladale and the Strath of Kildonan at the point where the railway parts company with the road; it is a typical small Highland railway settlement, with nothing more than the station, an hotel and a 'phone box, plus a scattering of houses as signs of civilisation. *Andrew Vines*

Furthest north on Britain's railways is Thurso, seen here in June 1977 with Class 26/1 No 26037 on the 17.39 departure to Georgemas and Inverness, surrounded by the trappings of a bygone age. The full brake coach behind the locomotive is probably loaded with mail and other luggage, while vacuum-braked vans stand in the bay platform and the still functioning goods yard. The timetable allowed for mixed trains between Georgemas Junction and Thurso. *Les Nixon*

Until the early 1980s the Far North line benefited from a regular wagonload-freight service. Class 26/1 No 26021 stands at Forsinard with the daily train from Inverness to Wick, waiting to cross the mid-day southbound passenger working, on 1 June 1977. In recent years, despite some gains for the railway, freight traffic has fluctuated markedly on the Far North line. *Les Nixon*

Impressions of the Kyle line (1): Early-morning light reflects Class 37/4 No 37402 *Oor Wullie* and the first train of the day from Kyle in the still waters of Loch a'Chuilinn near Achanalt on 4 September 1993. The shadowy hill behind is Sgurr a'Choire Rainich, a lone sentinel among the rolling moors which keeps the train company east of Achnasheen. *Hugh Dady*

Impressions of the Kyle line (2): Crossing the wild uplands from west to east amid threatening clouds, Class 37/4 No 37421 and its evening train from Kyle are illuminated by a brief patch of sunlight beside Loch Gowan on 11 July 1987.
Antony Guppy

Left: Achnasheen effectively acts as the mid-point of the Kyle line, where the time-honoured ritual of crossing trains has taken place for decades. Here No 37156 *British Steel Hunterston*, hauling the eastbound 'Royal Scotsman', waits in the up loop to cross a westbound working on 16 May 1992. The Kyle line was the first to employ radio signalling, or radio electronic token block, introduced on an experimental basis in 1984. In the following four years it was extended to the Far North and West Highland lines, but not without problems, chiefly because of difficulties in drivers' obtaining the necessary radio signals in the mountainous terrain. *Andrew Vines*

Above: One of the more significant stations on the Kyle line, Strathcarron is the traditional railhead for onward road transport to Lochcarron, Shieldaig and Torridon and at the time of this photograph surprisingly retained a manned Red Star parcels office. On the baking-hot morning of 10 June 1988 a rather battered Class 37/0 No 37260 *Radio Highland* runs round a permanent-way train after dropping ballast outside the station. The locomotive would be an early withdrawal, in August 1989. *Andrew Vines*

Left: Scenery on the grand scale in Glen Carron echoes to the sound of Class 37/4 No 37418 *An Comunn Gaidhealach* climbing through the mountains with an InterCity land cruise returning to Inverness in June 1988. The InterCity charter unit's weekend excursion stock, with its distinctive white roofs, commenced operation in the summer of 1986 and was a characteristic feature on the Highland lines until a hard look at the economies of the operation forced its withdrawal several years later. *Andrew Vines*

Right: Late on a summer's evening, Class 37/4 No 37419 hurries down the shoreline of Loch Carron near the hamlet of Ardnarff, between Attadale and Stromeferry, with the 18.20 from Inverness to Kyle on 10 June 1988. The coaching stock illustrates the standard Kyle-line formation of the locomotive-hauled era, whereby the full brake was usually marshalled in the middle to aid the loading of mail from the bottom of the vehicle ramp at Kyle, which is sited mid-way along the platform. *Andrew Vines*

Below: The gorse in bloom near Portchullin nicely complements the 'Dutch' livery of Class 37/0 No 37153 heading the 10.15 Inverness–Kyle service on 30 May 1992. The distinctive rake of green-and-cream coaches was introduced in 1989, although the associated observation saloon, converted from a Metro-Cammell DMU trailer, first appeared a couple of years earlier, initially in blue-and-grey livery. *Andrew Vines*

Right: Making a cautious passage around the shoreline of Loch Carron near Attadale, No 37418 *An Comunn Gaidhealach* ('The Gaelic Society') heads an InterCity 'Highlander' excursion on 5 June 1988. *Andrew Vines*

The Kyle line in winter, when trains are short and passengers are few: No 37418 *An Comunn Gaidhealach* is pictured *(below)* passing the inlet of Port Cam hauling the 11.30 Kyle–Inverness on 14 February 1987, whilst *(left)* No 37415 is seen near Drumbuie on the 10.15 from Inverness, also in February 1987. Port Cam, near Drumbuie, was proposed in the early 1970s as the location for an oil-rig-construction base but was subsequently dropped in favour of a site on the north shore of Loch Kishorn, marked by the distant rigs visible in the picture opposite.

The building of this installation weighed heavily in the decision to save the line from closure and led to the use of the railway to import materials via new sidings at Strome Ferry. The traffic was never as heavy as originally hoped, and by the date of these pictures the Kishorn site had closed. However, it did stall the case for closure, allowing the Kyle line to survive into more enlightened times.
Andrew Vines

Classic Kyle line: hauling the 10.15 Inverness–Kyle service on 16 May 1992,
Class 37/4 No 37407 *Loch Long* crosses the inlet at Fernaig, west of Strome Ferry.
Andrew Vines

The full range of the Cuillins of Skye opens up behind No 37418, three miles out of Kyle near Drumbuie, with the eastbound 'Royal Scotsman' on 11 June 1988. The train, which commenced operation in May 1985, comprises the original coaching stock in its attractive LNWR-style livery. After five seasons' operation these coaches briefly formed the stock of a competing luxury service, the 'Queen of Scots', which ran to a broadly similar itinerary. *Andrew Vines*

The clock was turned back on the Kyle line in the summer of 1993 when two Class 26s, Nos D5300 and D5301 *Eastfield*, repainted the previous year into green livery, were given a regular passenger turn over the peak holiday period. They were allowed out only on Wednesdays, thus ensuring they hardly ever ran in favourable weather, but on the evening of 25 August the clouds parted. The pair are pictured here at Badicaul, just outside Kyle, with the 17.05 return working to Inverness. *Hugh Dady*

All quiet at Kyle of Lochalsh on a winter's night in February 1987. Class 37/4 No 37415 stands beside the jetty with the stock for tomorrow's early-morning departure to Inverness. *Andrew Vines*

For many visitors to the Highlands the railways are merely a passport to the even greater scenic delights which lie beyond. The Cuillins of Skye beckon across the waters of the Inner Sound as the last train of the day from Kyle, led by Class 37/4 No 37421, heads back towards Inverness past Erbusaig Bay on 25 May 1990. *Andrew Vines*